Praise for Ricardo Sternberg

"Able to write on almost any subject from thumbs to ants and Spinoza, [Sternberg] writes with humour and grace, both exiled and at home in the world of language."
ROSEMARY SULLIVAN

"Always fresh and sensuous, full of the seductive rhythms he delights in teaching a reader to enjoy, Ricardo Sternberg's poems dance the steps of an earthly muse, traveling from south to north. In poems that would do Elizabeth Bishop proud, he brings Brazil to Canada in lines so intimate you will feel each lyric is designed for your ears alone."
MOLLY PEACOCK

"Sternberg is maybe the very best love poet writing in this country."
THE NATIONAL POST

"We are in the presence of a fanciful imagination who can weave myth and mystery into a colorful, exotic and sometimes erotic web of poetic intrigue."
BRITISH JOURNAL OF CANADIAN STUDIES

"Sternberg infuses his verse with original imagery that charms the reader and inspires wonder, elevating the commonplace to the magical. Carrots nail down fields, a lettuce leaf becomes the shroud of an expired mouse,
a broom whispers."
THE GLOBE AND MAIL

"These poems celebrate mind and body, sacred and profane, with an urbane and infectious enthusiasm that is highly endearing. Here are poems for all tastes."
CANADIAN BOOK REVIEW

"Charm in the deeper, original sense of talismans and magic, of sinuous, enchanting syntax and strange, brilliant images; poems infused with feeling for what Theodore Roethke called 'all things innocent, hapless, forsaken.'"
CANADIAN FORUM

"Sternberg is not stiff or banal like some of the contemporary formalists: like the trapeze artist in one of his love poems, he makes the work appear effortless."
MONTREAL REVIEW OF BOOKS

"Serene, yet balanced always on the hinge where surprise and conviction are simultaneous, with this book Sternberg reminds us that there are winds that blow from the world of dream, then whorled in the ear of a superb poet, freshen the real."
DON MCKAY

One River

SELECTED AND NEW POEMS

Ricardo Sternberg

THE POETRY IMPRINT AT VÉHICULE PRESS

Published with the generous assistance of the Canada Council
for the Arts, the Canada Book Fund of the Department of
Canadian Heritage

Signal Editions editor: Carmine Starnino
Cover design by David Drummond
Photo of author by Rosa Sarabia
Copyedited by Sariah Hossein
Typeset in Minion and Filosofia by Simon Garamond
Printed by Livres Rapido Books

Copyright © Ricardo Sternberg 2024
Dépôt légal, Library and Archives Canada and
Bibliothèque nationale du Québec, third quarter 2024

Library and Archives Canada Cataloguing in Publication

Title: One river : selected and new poems / Ricardo Sternberg.
Names: Sternberg, Ricardo da Silveira Lobo, author.
Identifiers: Canadiana 20240381548 | ISBN 9781550656695 (softcover)
Subjects: LCGFT: Poetry.
Classification: LCC PS8587.T4711 O54 2024 | DDC C811/.54—dc23

Published by Véhicule Press, Montréal, Québec, Canada

Distribution in Canada by LitDistCo
www.litdistco.ca

Distribution in US by Independent Publishers Group
www.ipgbook.com

Printed in Canada on FSC certified paper.

To my friend Sheila Dwight

*And in memory of
Richard Sanger*

Contents

THE INVENTION OF HONEY

The True Story of My Life 15
Thread and Needle 19
The Invention of Honey 21
A Small Spider 23
Flamenco 25
The Alchemist 27
Buffalo 29
A Pelican in the Wilderness 30
Gifts 32
Tia 33
From a Line of Ruben Dário 36
Reinventing the Wheel 38
Crooked Sonnets 40
A Note to Fat Frogs 43
Pig 44
Ana-Louca 45
The Snail 46

MAP OF DREAMS

No sooner had we left 51
What was left us 53
She was carved in Hamburg 54
A pig-iron disposition 56
You could say Gonzago 57
Blessed be the life force 59
A barbed rusty hook 61
Held to a diet 63
We had all seen dark rings 65

I, Diogo, son of Juan 67
The first signs we see are 69
Dawn. An arc of light 71
Across the arch of centuries 72
The island I searched for 73

BAMBOO CHURCH

Two Wings 77
Paulito's Birds 78
Parable 80
Mule 81
Florida 83
The Ant 85
Trapeze 87
Nice 89
Blue Letters 90
Tomatoes 92

SOME DANCE

An Invocation of Sorts 97
New Canaan 98
Pairings 101
Blues 103
Meal 104
No Love Lost 105
Ars Longa, Vita Brevis 108
Fishing 110
The Good Brazilian 112
A Prince's Soliloquy 114
Kings 115
Manual 117
Some Dance 119

NEW POEMS

One River 123
Midwinter Spring 124
Hogs 126
Sheeraz 129
Aubade 131
Mother Tongue 132
She Killed Tarzan 133
Easter Island 139
The Guest 141
Question and Answer 143
Mother-in-Law 144
Rivers 145
Las Golondrinas 148
La Donna è mobile 149
Delay 150

ACKNOWLEDGEMENTS 152

THE INVENTION OF HONEY

*"O Socrates, the world cannot for an instant
endure to be only what it is."*

PAUL VALÉRY

The True Story of My Life

At the age of three
I was promised in marriage
to a neighbouring princess
and took to heart
my father's interests.

As prescribed by her religion
I immediately underwent
strange rites of purification,
submitting myself to an awkward diet
of eggs laid under a waxing moon.

I was apprenticed
to seven masters
who, through a painful
pedagogical process
much in vogue in those days

though later discredited,
instructed me in the arts
of etiquette, fencing,
ballroom dancing, history,
archery, rhetoric and erotics.

She arrived from Vienna,
my dancing teacher;
a woman who despite
her advanced age and weight
glided gracefully into my life.

Beaming at me
from behind thick glasses
the Viennese was thorough
and ours was a tour
of what the world's feet
had been doing across the ages.

She was, however, prejudiced
against all modern movements:
the grotesque stomp of savages.
So what I learned and polished
were the saraband, the minuet,
the gavotte, pavane and quadrille.

But most difficult,
demanding the greatest grace,
the courtship dance:
a complicated series of gestures,
a slow, erotic posturing,
and finally the chaste embrace
of bride and groom.

One master enchanted me.
He was a one-eyed gypsy
who ingratiated himself
into my father's household
by magically removing
the unseemly wart
that blemished my sister's
happiness, my father's
designs on another kingdom.

His lessons were to provide me
with what my father called
Personal Magnetism.
I was made to meditate forever
on the cryptic remark
with which he would leave me:
*self-maintenance is the smallest
duty of the human species.*

With another master
I spent long hours
untangling the snarled
lineage of the girl;
but the incestuous lines
crossed so often,
their imagination for names
was so limited,
that I grew confused, lost appetite
and though severely punished
gave up that line of study,
satisfied that she was indeed
the issue of man and woman.

The princess herself
I never saw, though photographs
were sent daily from the palace:
a pale, frightened girl at first
and later, the sneering beauty
astride her stallion.

She would send me perfumed notes
recounting the exploits
of her favourite pet: *Today,*

she would write of the alligator,
he snapped a hummingbird
clean out of the air.

My twentieth year
was entirely devoted
to the study of a groom's
manner on the wedding night.

Instructed in the secrets
of zippers, buttons, clasps and snaps
my hands acquired the instinct
of searching always for flesh:

Of unbuttoning, unzipping,
unclasping, unfastening,
bypassing at any rate
cloth that stood in the way.

At the age of twenty-one
I sent the princess
three red roses and a note that read:
Je regrette;
I robbed my father's coffers,
eloped with the middle daughter
of the pastry cook.

Thread and Needle

Stern, starched, mustachioed,
my great-uncle spent the days
policing the stones in his garden,
the mangoes on his trees.
He spoke to me of the emperor.

Sinhazinhá, my aunt, the seamstress,
purblind with cataracts at sixty-five,
would hand me the needle and ask:
child, thread this for me.

If I moved my head a certain way,
Sinhá was inside the aquarium,
lost among the ferns,
sewing and muttering prayers,
oblivious to bright fish
threading in and out of her hair.

> *Silver needle, golden thimble*
> *I will sew your bride her dress.*

Sanctuary of boredom, that house
was a world, a system complete,
self-sufficient as the aquarium.

So who was it that interfered,
introducing into the house
a device that could thread needles?

I no longer remember.
But soon after I touched it
the contraption would not work
or would not work as well
and Sinhá, suspecting
a demon in those gears,
turned her eyes towards one
lost inside the aquarium
and asks, again and again:
child, thread this for me.

The Invention of Honey

Admit
from the start:
next to nothing
is what we know
about the bee.

Some have argued
that the sun cried:
the tears fell,
they took wings,
took heart and went to work.

Others have called this
poetry –
dismissing it
as hatched by men
with their heads
in the moon:
the bee is an ant
promoted for good behaviour,
given wings, a brighter suit
and the key to honey.

Very well.
The debate continues
and I do not know.

The bee is to me
as I must seem to her:
a complete mystery.

Small engines running on honey

Striped angels who fell for sweetness

Stars shooting into the corolla of a petalled sun

A Small Spider

Only a spider, a small
missionary of sadness
I swallowed somehow
when I was distracted.

Laughter broke easily
her thin restraints,
the delicate geometry
of the nets,

but, patient architect,
she drew more lines,
reinforced the structure
until laughter ceased.

Only a small spider
who came in one day
of rain or of sunshine,
one day like any other.

Tongue-tied, moans
were all I mustered:
lugubrious songs,
crippled lullabies.

Only a small sadness
on eight legs,
an implacable seamstress
with black thread

busy behind my eyes,
but day by day
the day becomes
more like night.

Flamenco

The guitarist must be able
without leaving the stage
to hang one of the strings
from the moon.

Any moon will do
but the guitarist who snares
a full-blooded one
carries the obvious advantage.

This awakens in the wood,
smooth and varnished,
the sap of its tree –
and this tree,

feeling itself hollow
throws out into the night
a lament as lovely
as it is piercing.

His fingers must be pure,
forgetting what they know
so as to learn
a tune beyond themselves.

Only then, his *rasgueados*
will quicken blood,
his *tremolos* draw tears
from the eyes of virgins.

At the sound of his *arpeggios*,
seraphim and archangels
descend on the stage
sweating profusely.

The music that is made
by the guitarist's heart
against the backside of the instrument
is contrapuntal to the other

and here it is superfluous
to speak of technique.
He must, however, be ready
and show no trace of surprise

nor falter in intensity
when his chair lifts from the stage
and floats above,
away from the astonished crowd.

The Alchemist

You will find
the laboratory
far simpler these days;
uncluttered.
The cauldron is gone,
the endless bubbling,
the stench, the maze
of pipes, the shelves
of exotic ingredients
that, however combined,
could not transmute
baseness into gold.
That is all done with.
Sold or given away
to whoever would have it.
The thin blue flame
went out.

But I have abandoned
more than tools.
The obstinate ideas
have been driven out
and I am now plagued
by something different
whose needs are simpler:
pen and paper and time
to apply one to the other.

There is no conjuring
but that which a pen
might drum
across the surface;
there is no incantation
but that which language
performs upon itself:
word linking with magic
word, the whole sustained
by the musculature of syntax.

Mystery is what remains
constant, mystery of magic
and of failure:
my nightmare of metal
forever dull,
replaced by this page
that remains blank
though I write upon it.

Buffalo

I have wrestled a buffalo
into this poem,
the least I could do
for an endangered species.

I have given him a tree
for shade, a stream
to slake his thirst.

A hulk of night stranded
on my gold-green pasture,
he shakes stars from his fur,
paws thunder into the ground.

The reader is to blame,
who brings red into the poem.

A Pelican in the Wilderness

When the woman with the mappa mundi
tattooed on her behind said, boys,
the world is yours for the taking,
I, for one, remained a skeptic. I knew

the rich got to the table first
and, once done, started on seconds.
The rest wait their turn, blue
with hunger, sucking on empty spoons.

Two occupations broke my father,
and I don't mean jobs. Then he fled
to the promised land, bruised
and burdened with an immigrant's heart.

He lives in America for Christ, work,
the bottle: sits on the sofa,
half plastered, Sunday mass on the tube
in a vernacular only half understood.

Once I walked into the room and saw
the old man kneeling on the carpet.
He bowed his head to a flickering
on the screen and then keeled over.

Every month the old geezers gather
to lick wounds from skirmishes
no history book will ever register.
After a joint, sometimes I join them:

The intelligentsia of the old country,
sweating in the grease shops of Oakland
alongside blacks and chicanos,
they, too quickly, learned to hate.

Before the night is done, as if on cue,
they will raise a silent toast
to Petras's letter framed on the wall.
Written before he was neutralized

by the NKVD, it brims with cheery news
but ends with this biblical non sequitur,
"We particularly like Psalm 102."
You might call it their drinking song:

I am like the pelican in the wilderness.
I am like the owl of the desert.
My days are like a shadow that declineth
And I am withered like grass.

I remember the morning he came
into my room; I knew something was wrong.
"Today is a sad day. Day of shame.
The Americans have published a map

no longer showing our beloved Lithuania
as disputed territory." And then he wept.
Our beloved Lithuania? It means nothing
to me except some names, photographs

and a territory staked in his memory
that stands between us and which I cannot traverse.
That drunken woman offering us her bum:
what else has history been this century?

Gifts

When I gave her smiles
she gave me a wooden bell.
I have never known such sorrow.

When I gave her some tears
she gave me a small drum.
Now the neighbours know my joy.

When I gave her silence,
the green bird she gave me
flew down my throat.

It is with his voice
and none other
that now I sing in sleep.

Tia

Of this one I now speak
but soft and low,
for I do not wish
to disturb her sleep.

Were my words to reach her
on that other shore
she would be embarrassed
to hold even this small
a stage. Her role
had been to always play
second to married sisters.

A fragile thing, she was
myopic, rheumatic, prone
to spells of dizziness.
Once, under the mango tree
that shadowed the entire house,
she began to fall but reached
for a trailing vine,
regained her balance
and, from behind thick glasses,
smiled at me: Tarzan,
she said and shuffled away.

A believer in icons
and in appeasing heaven
with prayer and promise,
she kept the household altar
outside her bedroom door:

a large niche painted blue,
speckled with golden stars.

Her patron was St. Francis:
a bird to each shoulder,
the wolf curled at his feet.

Paulo, her brother-in-law,
a feisty bantam, an atheist,
in arguments would threaten
to make out of that niche
a cage for his macaw.

In retrospect, I understand
those were rituals
enacted since before I was born,
meant to alleviate boredom,
understood, I think, as such.

As when, soaked in cheap cologne,
Tia drifted through the house
on a cloud of rose or jasmine:

upstairs rushed her sister,
then down some minutes later,
a moist hanky to her nose
to sit frozen in a sulk.

But these were exceptions.

Shuttered against the heat,
the house droned and they slept.

When I left for the States
at fifteen, she whispered
she would be gone
long before my return. And was.
But in my dreams she knits
a dream that has no end:

In a perfumed forest,
a parrot squawking on his shoulder,
Tarzan bows to St. Francis,
swings from a vine,
and steps to her back porch.

From a Line of Rubén Dário

"da al viento la cabellera"

With no dissenting votes
we gave to the wind her hair.
It brushes your cheeks,
now it brushes mine.

To the bee and to
the hummingbird:
her breasts.
We envy them the sweetness
that will be gathered there.

To the ocean belong
both her feet.
They will become
two inseparable
incredible fish
who may come out to leave
strange prints
beckoning bachelors
to walk into the sea.

We give the ocean
both her feet
and we warn you.

Many claimed her hands:
a tree wanted them
for fruit that would
be eager, for fruit
that would not wait.

A flock of birds
petitioned for her hands,
claiming that poetic justice
would be served were
       the feet in the water
to be echoed by
       the hands in the air.

We agree with this logic;
give instead to the tree
her ears
that it may hear itself
stretch and grow.

Reinventing the Wheel

It was no gentle thing,
the love that nailed me
as I stood perplexed
at the gate of winter.

Like some giant bird
that held me in its claws,
it shook the daylights
out of me and said look

look look, pointing nowhere.
My love for that woman
broke the gauges to leave
wide open the heart's valves.

The flood that rushed in!
You might say I was
in love with love itself,
and who needs the aggravation.

That whole winter
a flock of crows followed me,
dark notes alighting
on the staves of trees.

At night they rooted
by the warm chimney,
holding a gloomy vigil
over my restless sleep.

Here the reader ponders:
is this poet being coy?
So one-sided! Surely
a *few* moments of joy?

We reinvented the wheel.
Every pleasure was blessed
as we repeated movements
ancient and entirely new.

Her hands were small sharks
skimming the salt of my skin,
my eyes, explorers lost
in her sweet geography.

We were surf, waves, breakers
in the blue sheets of that bed,
while on the beach, crows
faced our turbulence and frowned.

Crooked Sonnets

I

Just when I thought
it was dead or dying
love, like Lazarus,
came back: summer,

the year I turned forty.
Once again it caught me,
rolled me under its wave,
threw me breathless on the beach,

spitting sand and words.
What does the heart ever learn
that it did not know at fifteen?

Incongruous discipline,
a sweet short circuit,
an unlearning is what love is.

II

Oh what a ball
once again to be
on the edge
of love and all

that jazz I said
goodbye to years ago
when all it got me
was not enough

and then way more
than I could handle.
With what impatience

lady, I wait to return
to the floor again,
to be by you set spinning.

III

Something akin to a sweet
energy traffics between us.
Have you not noticed it, lady?
I hear an erotic whisper

behind our words, desire
in convoluted arabesques:
reined in, raring to go.
Who knows if it's love, the flame

we hide and want to reveal?
Twinned power plants, our hearts
feed off each other and,

since love is distributive,
send the excess humming
to the grid around us.

IV

Your ups and downs, hesitations,
twists, turns, intricate manoeuvres
have, for the time being,
exhausted your dedicated lover.

She's had it with you, pal,
to put it mildly.
She's probably decked up some doll
to look like you and is this very moment

pushing long needles, barbecue spits
deep into its little heart.
Can acupuncture fix a heart that is broken?

Time can—or so sang The Righteous Brothers
back when I believed the simple pleasures were
and love was the brain going to sleep.

A Note to Fat Frogs

Nightingales fallen from grace
singing from amongst the reeds,
the stars, your inamoratas,
will not be croaked down
and you cannot leap that far.

What do you offer?
A balloon of ambition
and two eyes
that look at the world
moist with desire.

Grown oversentimental
you think you can woo the world
with your lugubrious melodies,
your antics on the darkened lawn.
Quick to jump

at flattering conclusions
you forget the world's owl:
literal, winged, hungry,
poised above you,
then swooping,

fat frogs.

Pig

One among us knows
the bliss of dirt.

One among us knows
the joy of bulk.

Unfairly rebuked
by visionaries
for lacking vision,
the pig I lassoed
knows it's useless
to poeticize the moon:
a bone picked clean
by starving angels.

A saint who trots
at ease with flesh,
his eyes scan
like empty plates.
He opens his mouth
and takes a bite
of his, of our
disappearing earth.

Ana-Louca

Antic-prone and crazy,
breast-feeding her dolls
through the streets
or on Sundays marooned
by herself in a pew,
she offered her litany
of curses and profanities
to no one in particular.

Thursdays she would come
demanding that which habit
had made hers by right:
the warmed leftovers
she wolfed down, standing
against the green backdoor.
Finished, she rattled thanks
from the gates and was gone.

A packing crate her bedroom,
she slept by the docks.
Amid rags and broken dolls,
asleep and for once, quiet,
a grizzled girl
lulled by the ocean's rhythm
as if cradled in its blue arm.

The Snail

Where is the snail going
and why the hurry?
Who is to follow
this silver trail
he dispenses
like a man
whose purse is broken?

I take it
the snail is a minister
without portfolio
officiating difficult disputes
between temperamental flowers:
explaining to the rose
that the geranium too
has a right to shine.

I take it
the snail is a garden impresario
convincing the marigold bud
that the time is ripe and
shyness apart, she must come out;
urging all flowers to their best,
then congratulating himself
backstage
on a successful show.

If he is seen at night
perfectly still
at the end of his shining trail,
if only his sensitive antlers
move,
the snail is dreaming
of some day
plying his trade
between the stars.

MAP OF DREAMS

Vera quae visa;
Quae non, veriora.

True, the seen,
the unseen, truer still.

No sooner had we left
the coastal waters,

the familiar latitudes,
than we were lost.

Rum-drunk, the captain
had himself blessed

and strapped to the mast
from where he begged to hear

something from the sirens.
Sail by power of dreams,

they crooned, *by ignoring maps,
by letting the helm go.*

When our supplies dwindled
we became desperate

and hammered our crosses
into crescent moons.

But neither cross nor moon
could replace the charts

the captain had destroyed.
We sailed as we could:

now for the sake of sailing
the silk sheen of this sea,

its blue susurrus.

What was left us then was the book
with its registry of monsters

(some imagined, some briefly seen),
its list of proverbs, the map of dreams.

Hairside to hairside, the pages stained
and gathered, the vellum bleached and bound,

fleshside to fleshside, into groups of ten,
the binding was of beaten copper, the cover

engraved with figures and hieroglyphs.
And within: each tenth page, a drawing:

In the first, sirens take delight
in the hiss and spume of surf,

alabaster throats rise from the foam
towards dark centaurs on the shore.

Open to the second and surprise the girl:
the glitter of gold is grain in her hand,

a sliver of moon is riding her shoulder
as she stands by a blue lake.

In the aquamarine of the last
an Amazon astride a reined dolphin

shoots an arrow towards a curved green coast:
my island the shape of a harp!

∾

She was carved in Hamburg
and given there the bright
blue eyes, the golden hair
and what the cook calls,
when prey to midnight funk,
her equivocal Teutonic grace,
for, oblivious to all entreaties,
she remains the steadfast one,
one eye fixed on the horizon.

Half her face is charcoal,
burned when lightning struck
in a storm off the Canaries;
others say no, not an accident:
torched on purpose by a misfit
who tried to woo her from the quay
when the ship docked at Calais.

The same holds for the tear.
They say it is but paint
carelessly dripped in Hamburg;
others swear that streak
appeared years later and at sea:
grief for Pedro whom, in fear
of the plague, we threw overboard.

Our glory is her hair
that frames her face in tight
gold curls then moves

to the intricacies of braids
only to be set loose at last
and flow back towards the ship
as if grandly swept by wind or wave.

A pig-iron disposition
annealed to a silver soul,
the boatswain kept to himself
except when a full moon
sat on his shoulder
and His Royal Gruffness
became suddenly blessed
by the gift of palaver.

Then it was the mermaids
adrift in our moonlit wake,
begged to be brought aboard,
there to sit, shivering,
arms around each other,
asking of the sailor
that he tell once more
the tale of Fergus
whom they had drowned.

And once he was done,
that he tell it again,
the grief in his growl
soaking each word,
until daybreak neared
and, singly, they slipped
overboard, to mingle their tears
in the salt of the sea.

∽

You could say Gonzago was born a sailor,
for his mother's water broke, or so
he was told, like a violent wave he rode
towards this world's harsh light.

And when that light fell from his eyes
he learned that to gather unto himself
the true wealth of this world
a boy need only rely on his nose:

by the bakery he stood before sunrise
for the glory that is risen bread,
then found his way to the slaughterhouse
for the smell, first, of distant fields
hidden in the hide of cattle,
then of blood-soaked sawdust and carrion birds,

and reached the market at its midday riot
to stand in a vortex of meat, persimmons,
freshly hewn pine, saddles, seeds, bolts of cloth,
smoked hocks, geraniums, chorizos, spices
heaped in baskets, dry beans in earthenware.

Afternoons that blind boy stood in the orchard
for the fragrance of orange blossoms,
at the creek for the smell of drying laundry
and of soap and sweat on the women themselves,
then at the barber for the oils and ointments,
at the church for incense and melted wax,
at the barn for the stink of chickens and pigs.

And at night, by his window, when a deep draught
brought him always news of the rocking sea,
he mumbled his prayers and gave thanks
for the feast given him that day.

∼

Blessed be the life force
teeming in these waters,
from that leviathan rising,
high as a church spire,
to the krill that feed it.

Blessed be the fish
in their prodigious multiplicity:
pike, carp, perch and catfish,
bluefish, herring, mackerel, cod,
the striped bass, the tile fish,
black drum, haddock and rockling,
the turbot, the brill, the halibut,
the sole, horse mackerel, the hake.
Blessed be the prodigal salmon
(both Atlantic and Pacific),
the salmon-trout, bonito,
barracuda, clownfish, monkfish,
the cardinal fish, the angelfish…

Blessed be all things bivalved:
oysters, mussels, clam and cockle,
and the univalved ones as well:
limpet, abalone, winkle, whelk;
blessed be the shy crustaceans
who hide their flesh inside their bones:
crabs and lobster and shrimp.

. . .

Blessed be the polydextrous octopus,
the shark and its predator's grin;
blessed be the steadfast turtle
lumbering up a moon-streaked beach
then regaining grace in water.

Blessed be all things finned,
gilled, scaled and valved:
all things moving through water
as we through the ocean of dreams.

A barbed, rusty hook
some fool left on deck
was waiting for him
when he stepped up
to his midnight watch.

It went through his foot
and would not come out
until they hammered the barbs
flush with the stem.
Bandaged, he hobbled on.

But five days later
foot and leg had ballooned
to twice their size:
blue, blue-purple, black,
the fissured skin oozed.

He was not allowed below
but slept – if you call
such thrashing sleep –
under a makeshift tent
built for him on deck.

He sat, like Job, patiently
washing his leg with sea water,
scraping scabs with a broken shell.
The captain asked for rum,
soaked a bit of rope

and made him bite it.
Five men held him down
when cool as any surgeon
the cook hacked off that limb
as if it were just timber.

We threw the leg overboard,
where it swirled by the ship,
trailing wisps of flesh
until a large fish came up,
lunged and took it away.

Held to a diet
of locusts and honey
a man could envision
the end of the world
in a shower of stars.

But this was rum.
Drunk and thumping
his holy book
the captain foresaw
a storm off the cape,

claimed to have read
in the tent of night
signs, portents, omens
of a ship breaking open,
prefigured as marginalia

on the map of dreams.
Though I hear nightingales,
smell the nectarines,
see honeycombs so laden
their gold overflows

in a long, continuous tear,
I fear I'll not set foot
on that green shore.
Rich in the rhetoric
Of grief and of loss

he exhorts the crew
to prayer and penance,
sacrifices to assuage
the fretful elements.
But to what avail?

When the waves surged
and he keeled over,
his eyes turned inwards,
his mouth a rattle of syllables,
we knew the ship was lost.

∼

We had all seen dark rings
round the sun, so who needed
the captain's mumbo jumbo
to tell us what was coming?
Still, such full-fledged violence,
unleashed so quickly,
caught us fully sailed and by surprise:

hammered by contrary waves
the ship would rise –
a bird swept by an updraft –
only to be plunged down, dropped
to the bottom of the trough;

the rigging stammered in the gale:
now taut, now slack, now taut again
until it snapped and the mizzenmast,
unsupported, toppled overboard,
but not yet free:

tethered still by a single cable
it trailed by the side of the ship,
a dog nipping but worse, a battering ram
knocking on the thin wall of the hull
demanding the sea be let in.

In thick weather the roar
of the ocean boiling around us;
everywhere the cries of men, their curses,
quick prayers whispered in the stealth,

the sudden shriek of wind-ripped sails,
the terror of cattle penned in the hold
and, over us, the broken covenant:
a black shawl of pelting rain.

∽

I, Diogo, son of Juan
and Catarina Queluz,
terrified, true enough,
by the sea that roils

and hisses round our ship,
but being otherwise
of sound mind, bequeath
what little is mine:

its dark sun ringed
in mother-of-pearl,
to my sister Angela,
my rosewood guitar.

To my brother, Luis
my horse, saddle and spurs
(the boots do not fit him
and go to my cousin Ramon).

My hunting gun, my dogs,
given me by my father
who also died at sea,
I leave to my brother Carlos.

The Catalogue of Grief,
The Romance of the Seven Sages
and *The Labyrinth of Fortune*
I leave to my sister Isvera,

but *Claudia Particella
l'amante del Cardinale*
is an evil book and so
I leave it to the bonfire

and ask destroyed, unread,
the five volumes of my diary
buried beneath the third
floorboard of my room.

To the pharmacist I leave
my stuffed Antarctic penguin,
my collection of fossils
and *The Healing Herbs*.

Green as her eyes are green,
green as sometimes the sea,
I give back to Marina
the sweater she knit me.

Let her each day undo
one knot until the whole
is undone: Let her then
turn away and forget me.

∾

The first signs we see
are birds: cormorants
flying overhead and away,
but then, as if startled
by our presence there,
turning back, circling,
squawking down at us.

Later that evening
close to shore, we suspect,
we hear a loud *thunk*
and feel the ship sway.
Peering overboard we see
the dark trunk of a tree,
rich with thick foliage,
each leaf now silvered
in the bright moonlight.

I can smell, cried Gonzago,
the earth clumped in its roots,
I divine a shoreline
fringed with green
to the water's edge.

Suddenly something leaps
and we all draw back:
already behind us, the marmoset
who brought in its fist
the crushed fragrance of the tropics.

We stay in the area
for days, keeping watch,
hoping for further signs
or the blessed shore itself,
but nothing else appears.

Were it not for the marmoset,
the trail of leaves it scattered,
we would have sworn
that under some spell
we had all but dreamt it.

Dawn. An arc of light
the distant horizon.

Our emblazoned sails
are ripe with wind

that take us nowhere
until Juan Garcia,

versed in the art
of the astrolabe,

turned his instrument
towards the sea

and brought us home
by drift of starfish.

The Indies? No,
we never found them,

but none of us
has ceased to believe.

∾

Across the arch of centuries,
the man in his hammock
—my great-grandfather—
constructing his empire
under the mango trees,

raised a lazy hand
and thus was I blessed:
not in prescribed sleep
between sundown, sunrise

but hard at work
in diurnal slumber,
on a hammock hanging
between the trees,
I put my shoulder
to the wheel.

Lulled by the music
of the busy and awake,
asleep but at the helm,
I redo Ricardo:

In the middle of the dream
there is a forest;
in the middle of the forest
there is a clearing;
in the middle of the clearing,
axe in hand, I stand
hewing timber for this craft.

∼

The island I searched for
is not there. Or has moved.
Or exists only in a space
circumscribed by sleep,
found in the map of dreams:
an island among other islands,
an entire archipelago
the exact replica
of a constellation yet unseen.

Perhaps one night those mermaids
had, as it were, overly sung
so that, seduced by their singing,
I could no longer tell
whether I was asleep and adrift
or wide eyed but forever fixed
to the stones of that quay
I had wished to leave behind.

No matter.
Behind the crystal of the bay
window, dawn had just broken.
Sunrise is that reef of light.
A soft grumble of syllables
and she stirs next to me,
returning as well from such
journeys we must undertake
on the way back to ourselves.

BAMBOO CHURCH

Two Wings

She would drift into the kitchen
trailing fragments of a hymn that spoke of God,
a river, the pair of golden wings
that would be hers on Judgment Day
and were you to look at her then,
you might well decide your best bet
for a meal would be to eat out:

she was blind and appeared a little lost
in her tile and linoleum kingdom.
But she vaguely addressed the garlic,
the onion, the tomato and between her hands
rubbed a sprig of rosemary over olive oil.
A fragrance then arose and you decided
you had best sit down. And you did.

Did you fall asleep? Did you dream?
You awoke to the smart snap of sails:
the billowing of a tablecloth.
She returned and a generous bowl
was placed in front of you.
Then she crossed her arms and waited:
her prayer done, your eating was its Amen.

Paulito's Birds

In dozens of plain cages
each with its mirror and bell,
my great-uncle raised birds,
but the steepled bamboo church
with a nest in its hollow pulpit,
he, the fierce atheist,
kept for the mating pair.

At his whim, admonished
not to speak, I followed,
acolyte with burlap bag
from which he doled out
ceremonious, almost sacramental,
feed to the fluttering tribe.

Half his thumb was gone:
a loss he would ascribe
—in a sequence meant to mirror
my own small failings—
first, to sucking his thumb,
next, to teasing the parrot,
and later, to being careless
around carpentry tools.

Perhaps it was his demeanour –
dry stick of a man – or the way
the door to the birds was locked
and he alone kept the key;

perhaps it was that stump of a thumb
grudgingly displayed when we sat
at the table and the stubborn
afternoon refused to move

that brings him back today
as wizard, magus, *bruxo*,
who, against ransom not received,
holds, locked in this spell
of feathers and birdseed,
the children of his kingdom.

Parable

Disguised as a camel,
the millionaire broke
through the gates
of heaven.

Brazen, that camel
brayed in the choir,
sang rough hosannas
out of key.

Good grief,
cried God,
and then stared
in disbelief.

But only when
down on earth
at the circus
a clumsy camel

failed to thread
the needle's eye
was the gatecrasher
recognized,

stripped of harp,
halo and wings
then sent hurtling
into darkness.

Mule

Watch it gain substance
as the sun
burns brain fog away.

Here is the brown field,
here, under the shade
of the olive tree, the mule.

More than gravity, *gravitas*
holds this mule earthbound.
Ages ago it said goodbye

to illusions. Today it dreams
of stones, sunshine, hay.
A no-nonsense clopper

with slow, Socratic eyes
too wise for foolishness,
too gentle for spurs,

it insists this easy gait
and a stubborn patience
will take us far.

We have barely begun
and, reader, already
you fidget in the saddle.

But who is to blame?
You were forewarned
and have no right

to ask this mule
to be what it is not.
This is no poem for you.

Close the book, then,
roll over and go to sleep.
Fashion out of dreams

why not a bicycle,
then pedal quickly
all the way to hell.

Florida

I

Grief came to a woman
in her dream of a nightingale:

the blurred image of her mate
resolved itself into a thing of fangs.

How sing under such weather?
arte povera, arte povera.

Rhetoric torqued to a whisper,
the lunar syntax of dispossession

stuck in the throat of the meek.
She strikes a rhythm off turtle shells;

she rattles seeds in a dry gourd.
She holds the heart to this thin diet

until it composes itself again:
sleek idler in the Florida Keys.

II

Solar is now the enterprise
that holds her to this dance:

a woman may rock back and forth,
back and forth, steady as the beat
of the ocean's heart, but not know
what brought, what kept her here:

aimlessness is an art and has a way
of getting you, always, somewhere,

but at the shore a woman quickly need
reinvent footsteps the tide erased.

Still, wired to the seasons
for this brief, singular moment

she sings for the sake of singing
this storm this engine this love.

The Ant

> "...ants have been growing fungus in gardens
> and eating it for millions of years."

As a washerwoman
back from the river
balances on her head
the loaf of laundry,

so too does the ant
return to the hill
encumbered
by a large crumb.

Such a hunger
could devour the world
or, from here to the horizon,
scribble a simple name:

ant ant ant ant ant ant

But more than a scavenger,
the ant is an agriculturalist.
Herself a minute tractor,
her fields the gallery

walls within the hill,
she cultivates a fungus,
a dark harvest
she reaps without a song.

Against the ant, tradition
holds this one complaint:
when winter rolled in
and its white artillery

blanketed the countryside,
she barred at her gates,
where it froze to death,
the jongleur of our meadows,

the improvident grasshopper,
for having fiddled away
the whole green season.
Food for thought to us fiddlers

(food for the ant come spring).

Trapeze

I go to her.
Sometimes
she comes to me.

Below us
the earth moves
as it must.

Hormones, hydraulics,
gravity, what not…
the quick arc

that takes us
from dressed to naked
in nothing flat.

But surely more.
Lost in celestial
ruminations, Rilke

told lovers to move
beyond the body
as if, in doing so,

they could enter
the locked gates
of a holier realm.

The metaphysics
of flesh and bones
and skin and hair

seemed lost on him
who could not see
that, fragile, transient,

perishable
though they be,
our bodies

are in no need
of transcendence:
moving together

they manifest
such power
as allows

two beings
to let go
the trapeze of self

so as to rise
—blessed acrobats—
fully naked

together from one bed.

Nice

Defunct though it appeared to be, they felt
the proper setting might make love return
long enough to lend to their finale
a touch of tenderness, of bitter grace,
a chance, who knows, at a rapprochement.
Thus, this little déjeuner sur l'herbe
with the oak as their sole witness
where they recall vows that crazy glued them
one to the other at Golden Gate Park.
Remember, she said, our weekend in Nice?
Nice is nice, he thought of the discarded
line on a poem left unfinished.
Recall, he asked in lieu of answering,
the morning I called you from an airport?
I was in Paris, booked on to Seville,
trying to sort out what it was I felt:
ten years of marriage and the heart's needle—
yours and mine—still wavering. You hung up.
At the bar at the Charles de Gaulle I sat
and drank, then changed flights and returned to you.
So you did. But what good were you to me?
A broken man who did not know himself.
Though I said nothing, I wished you had gone
to spare us both how many years of grief.
The bees hummed by a clump of goldenrod.
The wind ruffled the leaves of the oak tree.
The sun cleared a bank of clouds and shone down.
Nice was nice was how she remembered it.

Blue Letters

Dear Jody, I write to you
seemingly out of the blue
but not quite: I've read your note
which arrived by mail boat
only yesterday—a full year
since you wrote it, but I swear
I still see you late at night,
lining up the words just right,
losing track of all the hours
spent scouring the thesaurus
for new ways of saying "scum,"
on and on ad nauseam.
By the time your words arrived,
those feelings had been archived?
Or you simply let them go
realizing how their slow
corrosive work on the heart
takes its toll. You chose to start
anew. So why should I write
you now, angry or contrite?
Then again, I may be wrong,
knowing you can be headstrong
and nurse this grudge forever.
Either way, would it matter?
Halfheartedly, I wish you well,
knowing you wish me in hell,
or did so a year ago
when all that angry cargo
found freight in your billet-doux.

What of me since I left you?
I travelled—then settled here
and may stay another year
or two. I enjoy my place,
the whitewashed walls, the terrace
that opens to all the blue
I could ever wish. It's true
that indifference has not come
as it does, I'm told, to some.
Still, you're less of an issue:
these days I hardly miss you.

I write this on Saturday
while nearby two donkeys bray
by the soccer field where men
sit and smoke in darkened stands.
Through my open window:
the scent of mint, oregano.
Then, half song and half lament
—a lover who now repents?—
the arabesque of sorrow
rises from the streets below.
I may send you this or not.
What's the use of getting caught
in a pas de deux once more?
No one's asking for an encore.
Friends? No; but perhaps as ghosts
staked out at the outermost
edges of each other's selves
who slip in, sometimes by stealth,
or arrive, out of the blue
(literally!), and, typically, off cue.

Tomatoes

By dint of having to negotiate
the curved roads of the island, the zig-
zags of its mountain paths where switch-
back is followed by switchback
so the view seems continuously the same
but perspective is constantly altered,

a certain template impresses itself
on the mind: it too begins to rejoice
in the roundabout. And more: no longer
acknowledges the straight-line traverse
from point A to anywhere but delights
in the meandering any human exchange

such as this one affords: your purchase
of these five tomatoes, for example,
is contingent on your patience. So relax.
He will have you know that these tomatoes
were grown on land owned by his grandfather,
then owned in partnership by five brothers,

the oldest of whom was his own father,
a blacksmith, may God take pity on his soul.
One uncle went to Detroit, changed his name,
married, fathered two daughters, then died.
When the body arrived at the airport
and they opened the casket, a blond man,

impeccably coiffed, an American
flag on his lapel, grinned at the family.
They almost sent him back, they were so mad.
Another uncle owns the Christina,
that blue and white sailboat, big enough
to ferry forty tourists to a beach hidden

on the lee of the island. He charges
for food, for drinks, for suntan lotion.
He makes a fortune and drinks a fortune
and, twice, ran the Christina aground.
The fourth lives in a now empty convent:
caretaker, gardener and tour guide:

visitors ring a bell and he unlocks
the heavy gates, shows them the gardens,
ushers them into the coffered chapel
where they pray to a dark, ancient ikon
shaped out of mud and the blood of martyrs
or, foreigners, admire the murky mural

candle soot has over the centuries
practically obscured. The Second Coming:
Jesus, high on his throne, while on earth
graves spit out the startled resurrected.
The youngest uncle had his heart broken.
Lives now in another village. He's tried

to sell his share to the remaining two
but they can't see eye to eye on the price.
The land is stingy, he shrugs, yields little:
some garlic, wild oregano, but today
these five tomatoes and, coming round
at last to answer the question you asked

and one you did not, he negotiates
this final switchback to let you know that, yes,
the tomatoes are fresh and, hand to heart,
that, no, he could not let them go for less.
And five precious tomatoes, one for each
of five brothers, you suddenly realize,

are placed inside the bag and, having listened,
you are now implicated in his life,
in the life of this island that is criss-
crossed as much by paths and winding roads
as by the meandering of stories
eager to find themselves, reader, a new host.

SOME DANCE

An Invocation of Sorts

Niceties dispensed, muse,
give it to me straight,
intravenous, undiluted, right
into this arm I write with.

Here or hereabouts
(I'm never quite sure)
a show of modesty
is expected, so I admit

the gift is not commensurate
to the task at hand:
such a small wingspan,
my fear of heights.

So silver my drab tongue.
But as for theme: leave it to me
to come up with something
that, while not highfalutin,

carries a whiff of the sublime.
Finally, don't just hang around
after giving me my dose. Look:
I'm really, really grateful. Now adios.

New Canaan

I

A hummer, a whistler, a man
bent on keeping the blues at bay,
at the slightest peep from sorrow
he turns tail and runs away
lacking perhaps some enzyme
to properly process grief
as the mere hint of discord
throws him into such a funk
his passports are at the ready,
as are contingency plans
should he find himself again,
unravelled and unsteady,
but shouldn't he know by now
that as fast as he might go,
trouble hitches a ride in his pocket
and to prove it he might remember this:

II

The universe practically hummed
when they met and she said
we're standing smack on the fault
and my name is, guess what, Andréa
and this meeting has been foretold
to this very hour and day
three weeks ago by my astrologist
who dropped acid and his MBA
to train in an ashram in India

and was, you know, into stars,
for Venus was ascending
and Saturn transiting through
my second house, the house of wealth,
but she took wealth to mean just love
and that a van would be leaving soon
so, here, take a long puff on this,
and tomorrow, under a new moon,
they could both be in New Canaan
and would he like to come along,
and he said he would, and he did.

III

Everyone a vegetarian,
coffee strictly verboten,
the commune was not for him
and though he liked the sex,
he cared little for the hours,
waking up with the roosters
to meditate on an empty stomach
while bad breath and night odours
proved to be impediments
to the aimed-for transcendence,
insisting, as they did, the body
holds the spirit in a hammer lock,
and his the worst of all,
for as they sat down to their gruel,
his loquacious stomach growled
in such long, drawn-out sentences
he took to calling it Cicero,
and when sent into town for feed,

he was caught at the local Wendy's
and the camel's back was broken
for Brother Bill hauled him in,
asked him to leave, and he did,
with no time to say goodbye, Andréa.

IV

Unjust, this caricature of Andréa
drawn some forty years to the day
they met at the fault line,
for, in fact, he soon recognized
she had qualities he sorely lacked
such as, for instance, a backbone
he who drifted like a jellyfish,
and though she never accused
he sensed the disappointment
when she tracked him down
five or six years after Canaan
to find him stalled but revving,
running errands across the border
for the sleazebag, Doctor Ramon,
while she, after leaving the commune,
finished a nursing degree
and made ready to ship out
to work in a village in Africa
from whence she would not return.

Pairings

While a pair of Canada geese
peck at grass beneath his bench,
he faces Monterey Bay and lets
his mind meander, then settle,
on Noah: how, when the time came,
those pairs entered the oil-lit ark
still fragrant with the resin
of freshly hewn wood,
then settled as the skies grew dark.

Next he thinks of Flaubert's Emma:
after months of dilly-dallying
(the walks, the sighs, the long, long looks,
their eyes so full of serious speech
was how Flaubert described it)
she is alone with young Leon
unlacing her boots as the carriage
rattles through cobblestone streets
and, in its shuttered dark,
she moves away from her marriage,
giving herself, deliciously, to sweet Leon.

Then, a lifetime or so ago,
how they themselves
leaving a high-rise party
entered the lift in a fever
to hear Sly of Family Stone
sing he could take them higher
but stopped the car between floors
to have a go at it, oblivious

to a buzzer that rang and rang
and threats to call the police.

When the lift finally landed
they stepped into the lobby,
bowed deeply to the concierge,
then waltzed out hand in hand.
But just now, out on the bay,
a sea lion barks to its mate
and he's left with this:
O what a torture it is to remember
his nimble fingers, her firm flesh.

Blues

Toot me something on your golden horn,
he said to the musician.
I feel cold as my soul turns blue.

Jerry-build me an intricate song
full of those diminished sevenths
and enough thrust to push me through

bar by smoky bar into oblivion.
Extricate me from thorny feelings,
put brain and heart to sleep.

Bring out a flute and its Bolivian
so sorrow can be trumped by sorrow.
Afford me, at any price, some peace.

Today I am bedevilled,
befogged by this predicament:
will I find myself myself again tomorrow?

Meal

Asked to eat crow
he did so, and with such vengeance
he plucked the bird still warm
and from the collected feathers
made her a little pillow of nightmares.

Sweetmeats he set aside
to be braised in gingered port:
amuse bouche for another time.
He rubbed the carcass
in a film of olive oil and lime.

He nailed the handful of cloves
to his own chest in a pattern
that spelled her secret name,
then tucked the bird in a bed
of prunes and apricots,
flooded the pan with Madeira.
Later, contrite at the table,
the white flag of surrender
in the flourish of his napkin,
slowly and deliberately,
he ate the crow.

No Love Lost

Unable to string words tonight
in any manner that might please
he browses the mother lode
(what others call the OED)

by chance, Volume L through M,
and is immediately convinced
of the need to bring back
(banned to dial. vulgar and arch.)

the useful La!—exclamation
formerly used to introduce
or accompany a conventional phrase,
address, or to call attention

to an emphatic statement.
As in: He had a caressing way
but La! You know it's a
manner natural to poets.

Poets, when unable to write
(a condition known as blocked)
often drink, make bad companions
and should they drink excessively,

quickly reach labescency
(tottering state or condition).
They awake a loggerhead
(a thick-headed or stupid person,

a blockhead) praying a stroke
of magic or the next wee drink
turn them from loggerhead
to logodaedalus (cunning in words).

At breakfast, still under the influence,
they're prone to logomachia
(being contentious about words).
And the contentious word holding poets

enthralled through all these centuries
is love, found on page four-six-three
and refracted over several that follow.
The etymology is a complicated

web of meandering tributaries:
From OHG gilob: precious
to its Aryan root, Latin's lubet
(libet) pleasing, lubido (libido) desire.

Quickly, then, to the heart of the matter:
Disposition or state of feeling
with regard to a person
which (arising from recognition

of attractive qualities, instinct
of natural relationship or sympathy)
manifests itself in solicitude
for the welfare of the object

and usually delight for his approval.
Theologians, a further entry explains,
distinguish love of complacency
(approval of qualities in the object)

from love of benevolence (bestowed
irrespective of the object's character).
Then, among the proverbs, the sudden insight
that, mercurial as love itself,

there's no love lost between them,
meant first one thing, now its exact opposite:
so close were we at one time that in our traffic
there was no love lost between us,

but now, in the thick of lawsuits
and at loggerheads (two blockheads
making their lawyers rich) –
La! There's no love lost between us.

Ars Longa, Vita Brevis

Sitting upright, at his desk,
primed to begin work right after
this careful twirling of the pencil
round and round the sharpener
being oh so careful not to break
the unfurling wooden banner,
he brings up to his nose
to see if it smells of hewn cedar
and it doesn't, but just you look
such a lovely strip he managed
to make—but not to measure
since it breaks, and by now,
a plastic ruler in his hands,
what exactly he meant to write
has disappeared into the ether
so he goes downstairs and looks
inside the crammed refrigerator
where the carton of milk declares
itself way past its expiry date
which leads to an inspection
of all containers—in such matters
best to be absolutely thorough—
and what a mixed haul that yields:
yogurt, cottage cheese and ricotta,
but the jar of maraschino cherries
takes the prize, for "best before"
with a date all of five years ago,
in an open can, the tomatoes
are covered with white vellum,
the artichokes are about to expire,

time, then, to look for the recipe
his brother mailed him
calling for artichoke hearts,
pimento, mushrooms, green
onions and the zest of lemons,
which will afford him another go
at a long, lemon-rind banner
but the soft and wildly sprouting
potatoes should be thrown out,
and what about that Idaho senator
looking, they say, for hanky-panky
at the airport's bathroom,
and surely CNN could by edifying
but this Dalai Lama of procrastination,
as he was once called by someone
who knew the discipline it takes
to kill time, sees Topples, the cat,
staring unflinchingly at him
who, on the first of her nine lives
has all the time in this world,
and what could a cat ever know
about the state of a man's soul
but perhaps all she means,
is my water needs freshening,
and as he pours, he notices
the frazzled basil on the sill
could also do with some moisture,
but this man should get back to work,
and walking up the creaky stairs
he looks at his watch,
sees it is already four-thirty
so best he take a little nap
before his wife comes home,
best, in short, he call it a day.

Fishing

In otherwise beautiful countryside
I found myself at this fishing hole,
a shallow basin below a bridge
where the quick river slowed
to a sluggish, oily quasi-sludge.
The bridge itself, a poster child
for the nation's decay:
where concrete had flaked off
from the arched underside,
rebars showed a rusty ribcage.
The curve of three or four tires
broke the surface to hold back
a fringe of chemical yellow froth.
Beer cans and pop bottles strewn
over the ground where I stood.
Why ever did I cast? Boredom.
On my way home with no fish,
a few night crawlers left in the tin.
No sooner had I flicked my line
dead centre, under the bridge,
I felt the strong tug and struggle,
then reeled in a bright, large trout,
sleek and fully jewelled.
That such beauty could emerge
from such a waste of a place
conjured up a spellbound princess
who, as punishment for misdeeds
or, as often the case, sheer malice,
was turned into a fish
forced to live in this dump

until a prince—
I decided to keep the trout
and looked about for a rock
to give it a bop on the head
before laying it in the creel
but my eyes strayed over
the industrial decay of the place,
the toxic whiff of it all,
and so, most delicately,
I eased the hook off its lips,
waded into the stream,
releasing that quicksilver
right back into the muck.

The Good Brazilian

How, on those long afternoons,
when my great-aunt Beebee
sat with her sister Tia
(the two of them knitting)
and stitched together our lives
so that, dispersed, the large clan
gathered in the tent of their words,
did she ever imagine it would end?

And had they dropped a stitch
so part of our story unravelled?
The cousin taken by flames…
The uncle who disappeared…

Her son, Haroldo, my mother's cousin,
a man-boy my father's age
(an extra stitch in the chromosomes)
was shaved by Paulito each morning
before sitting down to breakfast
and the exactness of three buttered toasts.
(Changes, however small, undid him.)

Dropped into that household
every afternoon after school
(I was then seven or eight)
today I remember Beebee
setting her knitting aside,
peering over her glasses
as if to gauge the exact
degree of my intractability,

then wiping a dry brow,
turn to Tia and say:
Carolina will sweat blood
trying to raise this one.

Later, copying slogans Paulito cooked up
before heading upstairs for his nap,
Haroldo and I practised our penmanship
side by side at the dining-room table.

My clumsy scrawl was no match
for his ornate calligraphy
as up and down the page he boasted:
Haroldo é um bom Brasileiro.
Haroldo é um bom Brasileiro.
Haroldo é um bom Brasileiro.

A Prince's Soliloquy

Truth be told,
I wish she would
unkiss me,

turn me back
into the frog I was
and happy being.

Give me back nights
I dared the moon,
fat and round,

to step down
and skinny dip
until dawn.

My velvet britches?
This silver crown?
Nothing here even close

to those moments
when she dropped her cloak,
tested the waters

with her toes,
then slipped in and silvered
my dark pond.

Kings

King of Catarrh,
my next-door neighbour,
hails the morning sun
doing what he does best:
coughing up dead music.

This steady hack
and chain of whoops
are his attempts to drain
the bog that is his chest.

Once begun, the tractor
works a good two hours
clearing muck from roads
that, branching, reach
every clogged alveoli:
soundtrack to breakfast
on my side of the wall
or, today, as it happens,
to this chess game
where Luciano, I note,
left his flank exposed,
bent on a clever attack,
all flair but sure to fail.

I move a sly and lowly pawn.

There! With that harrumph
the King tractors through
some final blockage

and into his lungs flow
oxygen that is then exhaled
as song: his croak of longing
for the sun-drenched island
they all call home.

And now, my turn to gasp.
Lu himself moves a pawn
uncovering Episcopal mischief:
his black Bishop in cahoots
with the sashaying Queen.
Checkmate in two moves.

Manual

One way to do it:
occupy the white beach
of the page with words:
(supply interminable)
lay siege, then breech
by sheer volume
and manic insistence
the intransigence of silence.
Try to wrest
from the ensuing din
some garbled message,
then take that home
and mull it over:
i.e. revise, revise.

Or another tack:
grown abstemious,
to hoard the words
or dispense them
homeopathically,
slowly, one by one,
watching the circles
each makes as it breaks
the surface of the paper,
divining in the design
some hermetic message,
a truce freshly signed,
between word and world,
and having registered it,
consider the job done.

. . .

Knowing it is never done,
a provisional victory at best
that no sooner inked
proves ephemeral, obsolete,
insufficient,
the world (or is it us?)
refusing to stand still
so that what little clarity
is achieved quickly dims
as the word engine starts
again at the very start:
to stutter its way towards truth
or lies and be, at the end,
unable to tell them apart.

Some Dance

A little sauced,
you claim to hear
the music of the spheres,
and when you say

some stars are stars
that ring slightly off
as if the grand tuner
had grown distracted

or preoccupied or drank
too much at lunch time
and lost his perfect pitch,
I'm ready to agree.

This loss of pitch
is what you claim
makes the universe amenable.
By that small discord

it becomes more human,
as if that mistake,
if mistake it was,
brought *us* in tune:

we and the universe,
and after a dinner
where we drank
a bit too much,

standing side by side,
we do the dishes.
I notice the constellation
tattooed on your shoulders,

how the stars ripple
as if refracted under water.
You wash and rinse,
I dry and stack,

and then you turn off
the kitchen light and ask
would you like to dance,
and when I ask when,

you say now and then
turn to turn the radio on,
the music begins
and we begin to dance.

NEW POEMS

One River

This new me is so much like the old me
there's a chance you didn't even notice.
Mere passage of time proved no guarantee
when, stubborn, the self refuses change.

I've tried my best to learn new tricks,
yet find more comfort in the old groove:
howling at the moon like lunatics
do, mending the heart with needle and string.

I forgot that sometimes the broken
is as beyond repair as words
uttered that cannot be unspoken.
Who said you can't step into the same river twice?

Midwinter Spring

What sustenance
could ever these
imagined flowers
provide the provident
man who, midwinter,
facing a window
overlooking his yard,
yearns for a spring
hidden, to be sure,
below the dense
blanket of snowfall.
He's despondent yet
enticed to project:
under a canopy
of birdsong
come early spring,
armed with rake,
shovel and trowel,
he will, resolutely, go
to see just exactly
what winter—
declared to be
by resident realists
the worst in years—
wrought, then hid.
To make room
for that aspired green
he must, come April,
quickly do away
with dead branches,

dry leaves, spent stems
of long-gone flowers;
do away, in short, with
winter's trash.
Still at the window
and feeling the surge
of that sustained
if fictive spring—
sustenance perhaps
to last him the season—
he gathers a bouquet:
sunflowers, lupine,
pearly everlasting,
bog willow, columbine…
then walks away
to seek out a vase
exactly this size.

Hogs

Hard, at a glance, to gauge
whether the pig on this page

could ever go toe to toe
(be it in size or in weight)

with that other pig,
the one by Ted Hughes.

Here is the pig in question:
a slab of splayed flesh

dropped to the straw, snoring.
That other pig was dead:

a poundage of lard and pork,
too dead even to prompt pity.

Oppressed by all that weight
Hughes becomes all business:

How could it be moved?
And the trouble to cut it up!

Sylvia Plath penned a sow
in the blank sty of her page,

a grandam of glorious bulk
bred on the sly by a neighbour,

kept away from public stares,
prize ribbons and pig show,

a farmer's shrewd secret
kept hidden like a stolen painting.

Startled by the sudden backfire
of a tractor on the street

my pig opens a dream-dazed eye,
exhales a long, steamy sigh,

shakes both stall and barn
as it prepares to delicately

stand on sturdy trotters.
That hint of a smile on its snout

brings to mind yet another pig.
This one by Philip Levine,

being driven to market by a boy
and delighted to be on its way:

It's wonderful, it says, how I jog,
my massive buttocks slipping

like oiled parts with each step.
How to explain such good cheer?

Foreseen in chapter and verse,
it is not ignorance of what awaits:

It smells the sour, grooved block,
the blade that opens a hole,

the butcher's pudgy fingers
shaking out the intestines

like a hankie. Is it acceptance?
Or does it know something

about fate averted, a sacrifice
suspended, the timely reprieve?

My pig drops its tonnage
back on the straw and winks.

A smile blooms on its snout
and as it falls asleep it marvels:

what an inexhaustible
trough is this world of ours

whereat we feed and feed until
that day we are fed to others.

Sheeraz

Who does Sheherazade enthrall?
CHRISTOPHER LOGUE

Sheeraz came to my room, sat on my bed,
began to tell me some crazy story:
Rodrigo's dog had beheaded a chicken
and then gone missing. Rodrigo had
accused the neighbour whose chicken was killed
of having done something to his poor dog.

Done with my prayers, I wanted peace.
Wanting to fall asleep, I closed my eyes.
When I opened them, she was still at it:
Rodrigo had reached out to distant allies,
but so had the other side.
By then I was only half listening,

having noticed how artful nature had been
in placing that brown mole above and
to the left of her lips. I closed my eyes.
Her words became but a distant din
and I must have fallen asleep. I dreamt
of a man who could not abide conclusions,

who saw, in every story's end, his own.
Within my dream he came to see
that all the stories ever told
were offshoots from an original tale:
A woman undoes by night what she knit
by daylight, then starts knitting again;

a man forges small fish out of gold,
then melts them down and starts anew.
Caught in her silver net, his gold fish
escape only to be caught again.
When I awoke, wind rattled the windows,
Sheeraz was gone, her voice become the rain.

Aubade

What was then sung
was a dismal song:
armour plated (like himself);
the cactus cantata

with its choked melody,
its cutthroat words;
mouth shrapnel,
gruff gutter song.

To hear it once
was to be drained,
to wish day over
when barely begun.

Was it within the song
or within himself
he heard the rooster's craw
slashed, mid-crow,

as the bloody morning rose?

Mother Tongue

Save for singing,
how difficult now
for words to reach
my mother's tongue.

Beneath the stutter
you sense the strain
to bridge the gap
between synapses.

What the effort yields
is a rubble of syllables—
neither English nor Portuguese—
then frustration rising,

her stubborn silence.

She Killed Tarzan

(Décimas)

Cherchez la femme was good advice:
the likely culprit was Marie,
who was part Scottish and part Cree.
She had refused to pay his price;
instead, in ritual sacrifice,
had bled that narco from Seville,
then quickly thought perhaps Brazil
would prove the perfect getaway.
To live by Guanabara Bay
and linger there at least until

all hints of trouble died away.
But things took a strange turn that night:
her identity came to light
when her friend, Raven, joined the fray
and sabotaged her getaway.
Chinese cookie: do not ignore
a raven cawing Nevermore.
It was too late to make amends.
She left her parrot with a friend
and pinned a note to her front door.

Garcia spent that long weekend
puzzling the bloody homicide
but some time later would confide
he long suspected the girlfriend
but had no proof to apprehend.
Garcia thought perhaps a tape

had caught the criminal's escape.
When, weeks later, a tape was found
it showed Marie running westbound,
naked, inside a velvet cape.

The two of them had been in bed
when she reached beneath the pillow.
He drew on his cigarrillo
and next you knew it he was dead.
His final words remained unsaid.
She heard a siren drawing near
and felt the icy sweat of fear.
She spat at him her strongest curse,
then dropped the knife into her purse,
her goal to quickly disappear.

What came into her addled mind
was leave the California coast.
Her first ride, a continuous boast,
the second drove as if purblind,
craning his neck to look behind.
(It promised to be a long night!)
She felt herself wound up so tight
she could not sleep; took one Nyquil,
slept and dreamt she had reached Brazil
suffering through a bumpy flight.

Garcia coiffed his spiky beard
and wondered *how in heaven's name
am I to find out who's to blame?*
And worse was yet to come, he feared:
the evidence was spare and weird.
Save for Tarzan's, no fingerprint

but traces found of velvet lint.
The woman on tape used a gym
to keep herself in fighting trim.
Did these clues add up? They didn't.

He asked for help from Interpol
to identify the dead man.
Turns out his code name was Tarzan,
owned a rap sheet from here to Seoul.
Stabbed a Czech with a skiing pole
for making eyes, he thought, at Jane.
(A hot-tub threesome in Ukraine!)
He pimped and he laundered money,
claimed to own the Playboy Bunny
brand. Certifiably insane.

Marie risked murder, first degree,
yet stood by her initial NO!
The profit from her sale of blow
was hers and she could not foresee
sharing it with any would-be-
freeloading, piece of shit from Spain
(her words). Give in and once again
the dealer would demand they share:
what's his is his, what's hers is theirs.
A parasite on her cocaine.

Tarzan was just your standard brute
known for a famous hungry stare
that always claimed more than his share.
Her NO had been so absolute
she knew he would in hot pursuit
track her right to the gates of hell

or, easily, to this motel.
I had to kill him to stay free.
Alive, he would come after me,
or give my name to the Cartel.

The pool boy saw the photograph
sent around by the FBI
and called them from a phone nearby
whispering to someone on the staff:
The lady is here. In Flagstaff.
Garcia took the red-eye flight
with hope that he would soon recite
Miranda rights to a stunned Marie
who, unsuspecting, felt carefree.
A knock on her door at midnight

will bring us to the denouement.
The pool boy, Bruce, head over heels,
had parked outside his souped-up wheels
and asked her whether she would want
to drive from Flagstaff to Vermont
and lose the coppers on her tail
avoiding years confined to jail.
Yes, she said and again said yes…
I'm pretty sure… more or less…
She looked at Bruce and smelled blackmail.

She packed and then they hit the road
but as a pair were not to be:
as irritating as a flea,
Bruce's lack of confidence showed
in many a roadside episode.
Clearly a boy and not a man

when she compared him to Tarzan,
who had at least a little wit
while being a total hypocrite.
That night she dreamt of Yucatan.

She had a superstitious streak
and took that dream to be a sign
to quickly change the storyline:
when Bruce went in to take a leak
she simply vamoosed, so to speak.
Months later Raven got a card
of a dead crow in a graveyard.
It shook her, for she thought it meant
whoever knew would not relent.
Garcia's advice: stay on guard.

A year and a bit then went by.
Marie returned to Monterey,
a one bedroom facing the bay.
She met Luiz from Uruguay,
at an ACLU Fish Fry.
Head over heels he fell despite
the sense that something was not right:
nightmares where she would scream Tarzan,
her unease around policemen.
What would, he wondered, come to light

if she resolved to take a chance
revealing secrets from her past.
I know, sweetheart, you've never asked
Or ever looked at me askance.
She then stressed-tested their romance:
I killed Tarzan and did it so

He would not steal the next kilo.
His blood soaked into the bed spread.
It could have been my blood instead.
You now must choose: to stay or go.

A son of the patriarchy
Luiz was shaken by the news
and faced with her demand he choose
he walked his worries by the sea.
He felt he could not leave Marie;
not for the sake of...what? That hood?
It made no sense from where he stood.
They reassured themselves again:
Tarzan himself the one to blame!
Are we good? she asked. *Yes, we're good.*

Easter Island

In sea-fog
the statues appear
to weep:
long trails of tears
the rising sun
will soon erase.

But let's go back
to the beginning:
to evade purpose
you embraced drift,
practising
plain acceptance:

in sunlight
you thought sun;
in rain, you wore
rain like a coat.

Deaf to advice
except for one:
swallow nightly
the wafer of sleep
and dream again
the slow walk
up the gangplank.

You board the boat
aimed at evasion
but arrive here instead.   . . .

Those eyeless heads
monitored the tides
as they rolled in,
then rolled out.

The Guest

It has made itself again
from what it finds:
scraps of wood and rags,
an old broom and rusty pipes…

It binds itself together
with loose ends kept around,
and out of dank basement air,
it gives itself the breath of life.

It feeds on clumps of dust,
grows strong and here it comes:
we hear the heavy foot
fall on the stairs, the pause,

then the door slammed open
and it enters our life.
It wants to be family,
to sit at our table,

to sleep in our bed.
King of non sequiturs,
it holds strong opinions
and the need to share.

Experience tells us
it will be weeks before,
letting go its cold embrace,
it starts to come undone.

And so it is:
slowly on a Monday
it begins to fall apart
and, by week's end,

it is nothing
but bits and pieces
strewn throughout
our quiet house.

Sunday, on our knees,
with pail and patience
we collect what is there
and take it downstairs again.

Question and Answer

When she returned,
a determined look
on her wet face,
he assumed she'd
come to retrieve
something forgotten,
book or umbrella,
purse or scarf,
but what she said
from the threshold
she would never
again cross was
that, on further thought
(further meaning
what occurred
to her in, say,
the forty steps
that took her
from his door
to the bus stop),
she could now
flat-out answer
the question raised
when they said goodbye,
and then she did.

Mother-in-Law

She said she would get a whiff
of the goatish stench of Beelzebub
whenever the hussy entered the room.
That she feared for her poor son,
dreading the thought of grandchildren,
afraid they would arrive with tail,
cloven hoofs and that awful stink.
That she took to bringing along
a vial of lucky, holy water
and, for protection, dropped
the filigreed crucifix at her chest
for the heft of a bronze cross
that gave her a splitting headache
and now this permanent stoop.

Rivers

> Nuestras vidas son los rios
> que van a dar en la mar,
> que es el morir
>
> JORGE MANRIQUE

My father had insisted
he did not want an American funeral,
by which he meant: the cheerfulness
and the laughing at anecdotes
the living here tell about the dead.

No. He wanted throats constricted,
speech impeded, eyes rimmed red,
the room brimming with tears.
So I was unsure exactly
whose funeral I was attending,

but in the dream it fell to me
to place the LP of Piaf (or Brel?)
on a turntable beneath the bier
that held his plain pine coffin.
People milled about the church,

waiting for the service to begin.
Then David, a friend, himself dead,
had an urgent matter to discuss:
some properties he owned in Arizona
needed inspection and he wondered

would I be up for the ride west.
Whether this was the same current,
a tributary, or an entirely new dream
didn't matter, for it carried me
out of sleep. My father's funeral?

He was cremated. A mass held
at The Newman Center in Berkeley,
a reception at the Faculty Club.
A slide presentation brought him
from the time he was a baby,

helpless in his mother's arms,
to his last days: a geographer
who had lost his bearings.
Grief was held in check
but haunted my mother's eyes.

A month later my brother and his wife
took the ashes to the Amazon,
poured them into a small clay pot
bought in the market at Manaus
and went upriver to the Paraná,

near to where my father spent
a lifetime on research. Leo poured
the ashes into the river, sent us all
a note: Husband, father, grandfather,
great-grandfather no longer studies

the Amazon. He is the Amazon.
He told me that as the ashes
mixed slowly with the river,
a storm of bright, noisy perroquets
flew to a nearby branch.

I wasn't there but like to think
the bird racket rose as disobedience
and hope it followed my father
as he swirled all the way downriver
to the mouth of the Amazon

and into the ocean beyond.

Las Golondrinas

> *ésas... ¡no volverán!*
> BÉCQUER

Where, he asks, waking, are the swallows
of yesteryear, said to never return?
Everything else does! Grief, for starters,
with its fractal, endless re-enactments.

Or how our dreams find fresh ways
to twist the rusty knife
deep into the heart's meat. Even the dead
refuse to be done and, like Lazarus,

storm back, demanding redress.
Asleep or awake, is what remains
nothing but revision, this returning
to make right what you first made wrong?

La Donna è Mobile

He never knew what she'd do next.
Her every move left him perplexed
as to the nature of a game
where rules never remained the same
but morphed according to her mood:
Was she exalted or subdued?
He carefully weighed the cons and pros:
her pinch of poetry to his prose.

He never knew who would arrive,
so steeled himself to improvise
and play her appropriate counterpart
but lacked, it seemed, her nimble heart.
Give us, he prayed, our daily dread:
He called her Silver; she called him Lead.

Delay

Perhaps a cuff to the head—
think Paul en route to Damascus—
will prove to be his wake-up call.

Proverbial river, life runs and
runs until it runs dry.
Yet he waits. Defers.

Prince of prefaces and preludes,
rehearsing actions he'll postpone
again. Isn't now the time?

Tomorrow perhaps. Or the day after.
Best not rush into things.
He keeps in check that first step

while he lingers in the wings,
ignoring cue or sign that tells him:
Begin!

ACKNOWLEDGEMENTS

Earlier versions of some of these poems have appeared in *CV2*, *The Antigonish Review*, *The Fiddlehead*, *The Windsor Review* and *The Walrus*.

"Hogs" includes lines by Ted Hughes, Sylvia Plath and Philip Levine.

I am grateful to the editors of my previous books: Michael Harris (*The Invention of Honey* and *Map of Dreams*, Véhicule Press), Kerry McSweeney and Alan Hepburn (*Bamboo Church* and *Some Dance* respectively, McGill-Queen's University Press). Sheila Dwight and Doug Thompson have been helpful with suggestions on many of these poems. The first poem in this book was originally presented in Stephen Yenser's creative writing seminar at UCLA. He has been generous with editorial help ever since, and his suggestions have improved poems throughout this book. I am grateful to Carmine Starnino for suggesting this volume and for guiding it through the shoals of editing.

CARMINE STARNINO, EDITOR
MICHAEL HARRIS, FOUNDING EDITOR

Robert Allen • James Arthur • John Asfour, trans.
John Barton • Doug Beardsley • Paul Bélanger
Linda Besner • Walid Bitar • Marie-Claire Blais
Yves Boisvert • Jenny Boychuk • Asa Boxer • Susan Briscoe
René Brisebois, trans. • Mark Callanan • Chad Campbell
Edward Carson • Arthur Clark • Yoyo Comay
Don Coles • Vincent Colistro • Jan Conn • Geoffrey Cook
Lissa Cowan, trans. • Judith Cowan, trans. • Mary Dalton
Ann Diamond • George Ellenbogen • Louise Fabiani
Joe Fiorito • Bill Furey • Michel Garneau • Susan Glickman
Gérald Godin • Lorna Goodison • Richard Greene
Jason Guriel • Michael Harris • Carla Hartsfield
Elisabeth Harvor • Charlotte Hussey • Dean Irvine, ed.
Jim Johnstone • D. G. Jones • Francis R. Jones, trans.
Virginia Konchan • Anita Lahey • Kateri Lanthier
R. P. LaRose • Ross Leckie • Erik Lindner • Michael Lista
Laura Lush • Errol MacDonald • Brent MacLaine
Muhammad al-Maghut • Nyla Matuk • Robert McGee
Sadiqa de Meijer • Robert Melançon • Robert Moore
Pierre Morency • Pierre Nepveu • Eric Ormsby
Elise Partridge • Christopher Patton • James Pollock
Michael Prior • Medrie Purdham • John Reibetanz
Peter Richardson • Robin Richardson • Laura Ritland
Talya Rubin • Richard Sanger • Stephen Scobie

Talya Rubin • Richard Sanger • Stephen Scobie
Peter Dale Scott • Deena Kara Shaffer
Carmine Starnino • Andrew Steinmetz • David Solway
Ricardo Sternberg • Shannon Stewart
Philip Stratford, trans. • Matthew Sweeney
Harry Thurston • Rhea Tregebov • Peter Van Toorn
Patrick Warner • Derek Webster • Anne Wilkinson
Donald Winkler, trans. • Shoshanna Wingate
Christopher Wiseman • Catriona Wright
Terence Young